bored

 silly

 excited

 worried

 shy

 angry

 loving

 anxious

 affectionate

 dreamy

 guilty

 proud

 scared

 disappointed

 embarrassed

 unsure

ALL FEELINGS ARE OK –
IT'S WHAT YOU DO WITH THEM
THAT COUNTS

By Lawrence E. Shapiro, Ph.D.

Illustrated by Jille Mandel

D0906349

Childswork/Childsplay, LLC
Plainview, N.Y.

 upset

 shocked

 confused

 jealous

 brave

surprised

ALL FEELINGS ARE OK – IT'S WHAT YOU DO WITH THEM THAT COUNTS
By Lawrence E. Shapiro, Ph.D.
Illustrated by Jille Mandel
Play-and-Read Series Editor: Hennie M. Shore

Published by:
Childswork/Childsplay, LLC
135 Dupont Street
Plainview, N.Y. 11803
1-800-962-1141

Childswork/Childsplay is a catalogue of products for mental
health professionals, teachers and parents who wish to help
children with their developmental, social and emotional growth.

All rights reserved. Childswork/Childsplay grants limited permission for the
copying from this publication to its customers for their individual professional use. Permission
for publication or any other use must be obtained in writing.

Copyright ©1993 by Childswork/Childsplay, LLC
Printed in the United States of America
Third Edition

ISBN 1-882732-04-9

Other products by Childswork/Childsplay:

Play-and-Read Series Books
ALL ABOUT DIVORCE
TAKE A DEEP BREATH: The Kids' Play-Away Stress Book
FACE YOUR FEELINGS

Self-Esteem Series Books
SOMETIMES I DRIVE MY MOM CRAZY, BUT I KNOW SHE'S CRAZY ABOUT ME:
  A Self-Esteem Book for ADHD Children
SOMETIMES I LIKE TO FIGHT, BUT I DON'T DO IT MUCH ANYMORE

Psychological Games
MY TWO HOMES
STOP, RELAX & THINK
THE ANGRY MONSTER MACHINE
THE CLASSROOM BEHAVIOR GAME
THE DINOSAUR'S JOURNEY TO HIGH SELF-ESTEEM
THE GOOD BEHAVIOR GAME
THE GREAT FEELINGS CHASE
YOU & ME: A GAME OF SOCIAL SKILLS
LOOK BEFORE YOU LEAP
POSITIVE THINKING GAME
RIGHT OR WRONG
ANGER SOLUTION GAME
SELF-CONTROL PATROL GAME
TEAMWORK
THE ROAD TO PROBLEM MASTERY

For a free catalogue of books, games and toys to help children, call 1-800-962-1141.

Preface

Learning to recognize and talk about one's feelings is an important part of growing up. Whether in the kitchen or the classroom, the playground or the ball field, when children can talk about their feelings they are more likely to have their needs understood and met.

When children are given the chance to express and learn about their feelings, they also develop insights about themselves. When kids understand their feelings, they can learn to understand their motivations, needs, and problems.

Like learning to recognize letters, children must be taught to recognize their feelings and to understand what they mean. And we, as adults, must take the time to teach them.

And just as letter recognition is only the first step to reading, recognizing feelings is only the beginning of learning the language of feelings. Understanding our feelings and taking responsibility for them is important at every stage of development.

Accompanying this book are four different Feelings Faces stamps, which children will enjoy using to complete the humorous cartoons. Older children may want to draw in their own faces using the 34 Feelings Faces that are included on page 91 and the separate sheet, expressing more specific feelings. We have also provided a small package of crayons to color in the pictures as well, recognizing that many children express themselves in the coloring.

Under each picture, children may fill in (or grown-ups may fill in for them) the feeling that is being expressed in the picture as well as the question about the feeling that follows.

But these activities are just the beginning of how children learn about their feelings. Either during the activity, or afterwards, you should encourage children to talk about their feelings and you should feel free to talk about yours. Talking and listening is how children develop insights into their feelings, so make sure that you give them every opportunity possible to do this.

Remember that **all feelings are OK.** Children must learn that they are entitled to their feelings, whatever they are. **But it's what you do with feelings that count.** Children must also learn that even though they may *feel* a certain way, that does not mean that they can *act* on their feelings in any way that they like. They must understand that other people have feelings too!

How do you feel when kids tease you?

What can you do to feel better?

_____

_____

_____

How do you feel when you eat ice cream?

What else makes you feel that way?

_____

_____

_____

How do you feel when your father is upset?

Is there something you can do?

_____

_____

_____

How do you feel when you get a good grade?

What can you do to get another good grade?

_____

_____

How do you feel when you eat too much candy?

Can you think of a healthier snack?

_____

_____

_____

How do you feel when a pet dies?

What could you do to feel better?

_____

_____

_____

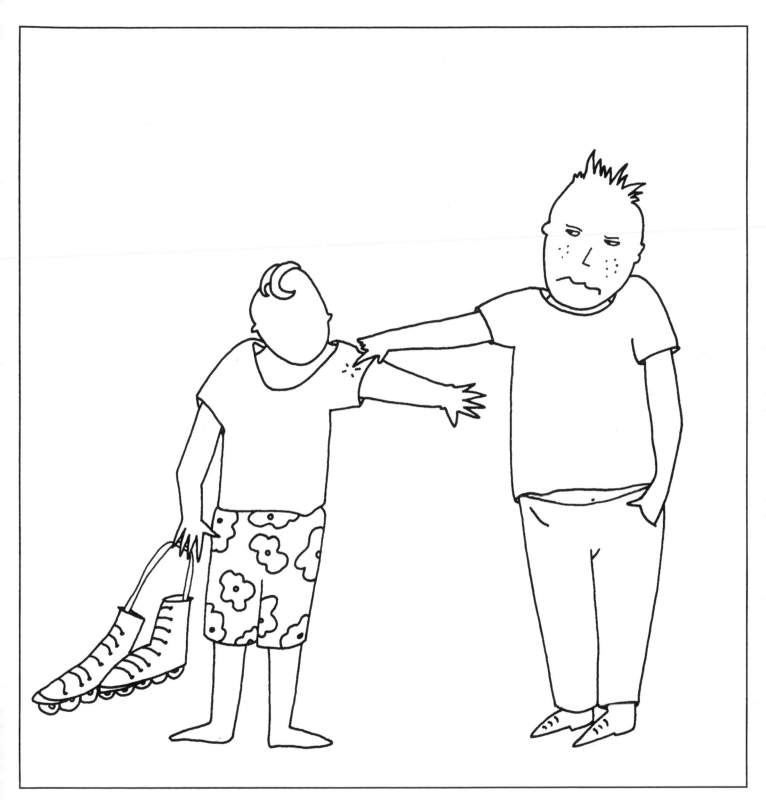

How do you feel when a bully picks on you?

What can you do so that he leaves you alone?

_____

_____

_____

How do you feel when you get a surprise Valentine card?

Why do you think people send Valentines?

_____

_____

_____

How do you feel when you see someone asking for money?

What could you do to help a homeless person?

_____

_____

_____

How do you feel when your mom makes you eat vegetables you don't like?

Why does she do that?

_____

_____

_____

How do you feel when you hit a home run?

Who would be most proud of you?

_____

_____

_____

How do you feel when you think about growing up?

What's the best thing about being a grown-up?

_____

_____

_____

How do you feel when you hear about people with problems on TV?

What could you do to help?

_____

_____

_____

How do you feel when you make your own lunch?

Why is it good to make your own lunch?

_____

_____

_____

How do you feel when your dad says you have to go to bed at 8:00 and all your friends go to bed at 9:00?

What could you say to your dad?

_____

_____

How do you feel when your parents argue?

What do you do?

_____

_____

_____

How do you feel when you read a great book?

What book is it?

_____

_____

How do you feel when your parents say, "No more TV!"

What do you do?

_____

_____

_____

How do you feel when your teacher calls on you at school and you don't know the answer?

What do you do?

_____

_____

How do you feel when you can't find your favorite toy?

What do you do about it?

_____

_____

_____

How do you feel when you get wet on a hot day?

What else makes you feel that way?

_____

_____

_____

How do you feel on the day before your birthday?

Does anything else make you feel that way?

_____

_____

_____

How do you feel on the day *after* your birthday?

What is another special day in your life?

_____

_____

_____

How do you feel when you're waiting for the dentist?

What could you do to feel differently?

_____

_____

_____

How do you feel when you lose a game?

What can you do to feel better?

_____

_____

_____

How do you feel when you don't do your homework?

What can you do so that you won't have to feel that way?

_____

_____

_____

How do you feel when someone has a crush on you?

Is there something you should do?

_____

_____

How do you feel when you stub your toe?

How can you make it feel better?

_____

_____

_____

How do you feel when your best friend says she's too busy to play?

What else can you do?

_____

_____

_____

How do you feel when you break something?

What should you do?

_____

_____

_____

How do you feel when you get your chores done early?

How can you make sure that happens?

_____

_____

How do you feel when you earn extra money?

What could you do to earn extra money?

_____

_____

_____

How do you feel when your mom yells at you?

Why do you feel that way?

_____

_____

_____

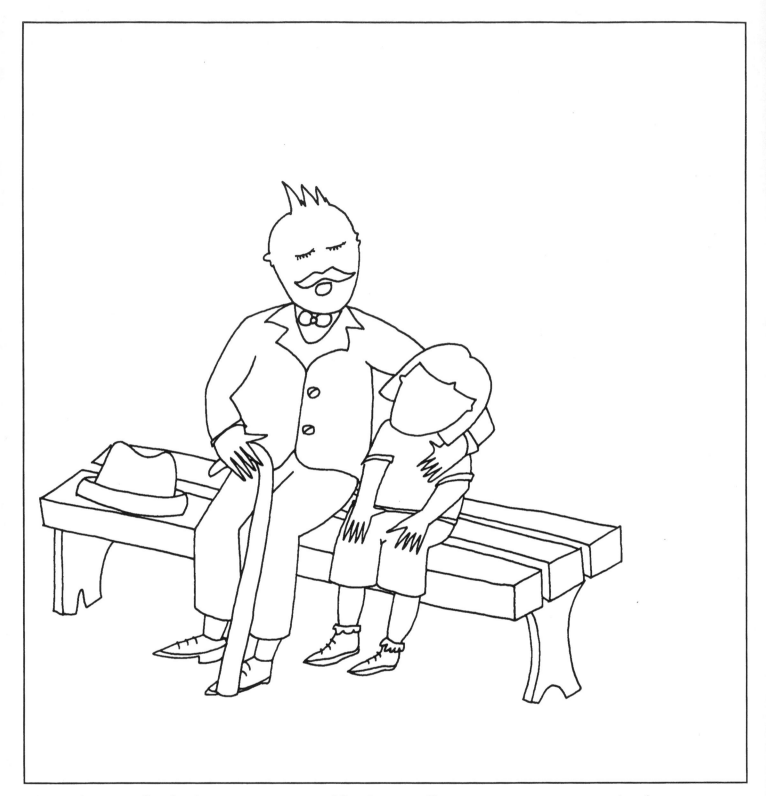

How do you feel when your grandfather tells you a story you don't understand?

What do you do?

_____

_____

How do you feel when you think about pollution?

What can you do about pollution?

_____

_____

_____

How do you feel when you see someone smoking a cigarette?

Why is smoking bad?

_____

_____

_____

How do you feel when you have a substitute teacher?

What do you do?

_____

_____

_____

How do you feel on the last day of school?

What else makes you feel that way?

_____

_____

_____

How do you feel on the 4th of July?

What's your favorite holiday?

_____

_____

How do you feel when you wake up on a stormy night and there is thunder and lightning?

Who could help you feel better?

_____

_____

How do you feel when your mother is crying?

What can you do?

_____

_____

_____

How do you feel when you take something that doesn't belong to you?

What could you do to make things better?

_____

_____

_____

How do you feel if your friend has a party and you're not invited?

Could you do anything to make yourself feel better?

_____

_____

_____

How do you feel if your mom pays more attention to another child than to you?

Why do you feel that way?

_____

_____

How do you feel when a grown-up hits you?

What can you do about it?

_____

_____

_____

How do you feel if you are lost in a big store?

Who can help you?

_____

_____

_____

How do you feel if a huge dog comes over to you?

What should you do?

_____

_____

_____

How do you feel if someone accidentally breaks your favorite toy?

What can you do about it?

_____

_____

_____

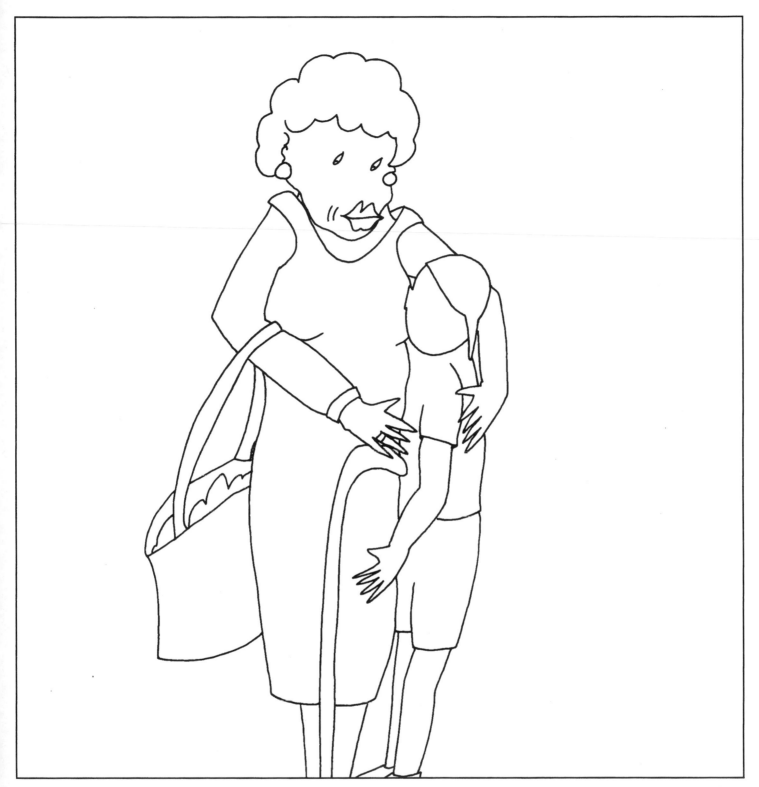

How do you feel when your grandmother wants to give you a big kiss?

How do you think she feels?

_____

_____

_____

How do you feel if someone important forgets your birthday?

What can you do about it?

_____

_____

_____

How *do* you feel if someone at school takes the lunch your mom made for you?

What can you *do* about it?

_____

_____

How do you feel when your dad spends the whole afternoon just with you?

What would you say to him?

_____

_____

_____

How do you feel when you think of yourself being grown up?

Why do you feel that way?

_____

_____

_____

How do you feel when you are playing basketball and everyone else is taller?

Is there anything you can do about it?

_____

_____

_____

How do you feel if you are just about to dive from a very high diving board?

Why do you feel that way?

_____

_____

_____

How do you feel when you know you've broken an important rule?

What can you do about it?

_____

_____

_____

How do you feel when the teacher yells at you for passing a note, but you didn't do it?

What can you do about it?

_____

_____

_____

How do you feel when you solve a problem that was really hard?

When did this happen?

_____

_____

_____

How do you feel when your mom looks like she had a really bad day?

What can you do?

_____

_____

_____

How do you feel when your favorite song comes on the radio?

Why does it make you feel that way?

_____

_____

_____

How would you feel if a genie gave you one wish?

What would it be?

_____

_____

_____

How do you feel when you are waiting in a very long line?

What can you do about it?

_____

_____

_____

How do you feel when you're waiting for your lunch, and you're really hungry, and when it comes there's a big bug in it?

What can you do?

_____

_____

_____

How do you feel when your uncle pinches your cheek really hard and says, "You're soooo cute!"

What would you say?

_____

_____

_____

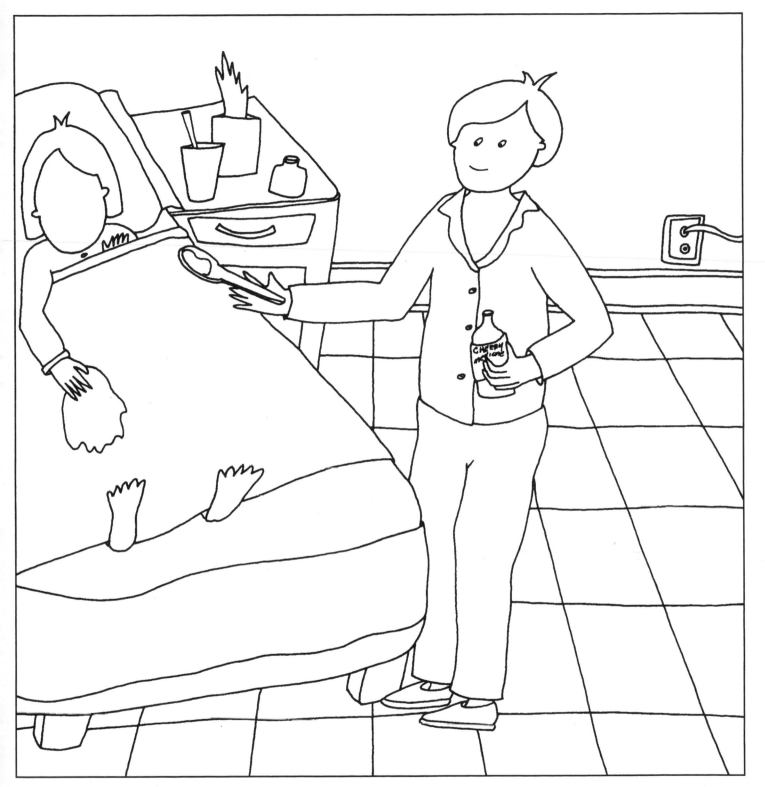

How do you feel when you've got a bad cold and your dad makes you take bad-tasting medicine?

What can you do?

_____

_____

_____

How do you feel when you get to school and realize that you forgot the project you were supposed to bring?

What can you do about it?

_____

_____

_____

How do you feel when you lose your lunch money?

What can you do?

_____

_____

_____

How do you feel when you really have to get to school on time and your mom is running *really* late?

Is there anything you can *do* to help her get ready?

_____

_____

_____

How do you feel when teams are being chosen for kickball and you're the last one picked?

What can you do?

_____

_____

_____

How do you feel when you have to do your homework and your favorite TV program is on?

What can you do so that it doesn't happen again?

_____

_____

_____

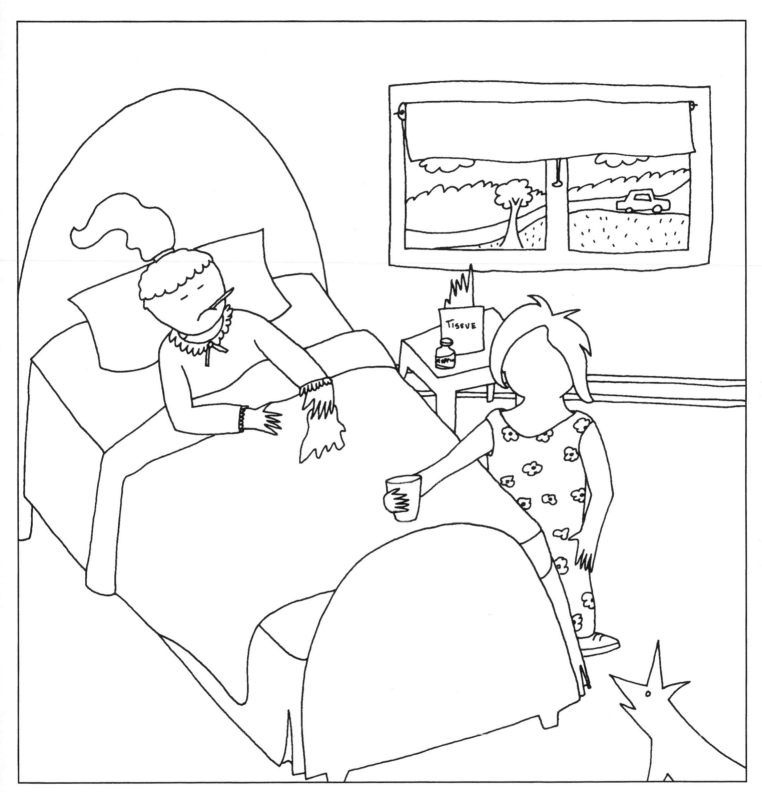

How do you feel when your mom isn't feeling well?

What can you do?

_____

_____

_____

How do you feel when your best friend is angry at you?

What can you do about it?

_____

_____

_____

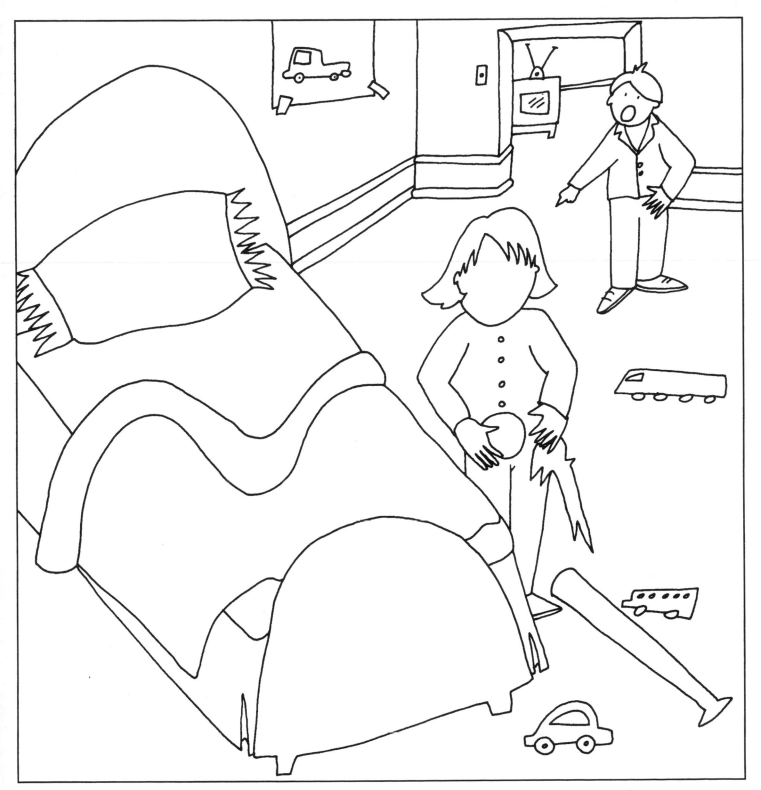

How do you feel when you have to go to bed but you're not tired?

What can you do to relax and feel sleepy?

_____

_____

_____

How do you feel when you're punished?

What can you do?

_____

_____

_____

How do you feel when you're drawing a picture but it's not turning out the way you want?

What can you do?

_____

_____

How do you feel when it's a beautiful spring day?

What else makes you feel that way?

_____

_____

_____

How do you feel when you see an animal that's been hurt?

What can you do?

_____

_____

_____

How do you feel when you draw a beautiful picture?

Where will you hang it?

_____

_____

_____

How do you feel when you go to a museum?

What's another place that makes you feel that way?

_____

_____

_____

How do you feel when your family goes on a long car trip?

Why do you feel that way?

_____

_____

_____

How do you feel when your dad comes home from work in a bad mood?

What can you do?

_____

_____

_____

How do you feel when you tell a really funny joke and nobody laughs?

What can you do?

_____

_____

_____

How do you feel when your mom tells you she has to go on a long business trip?

Why do you feel that way?

_____

_____

_____

How do you feel when you're chosen for the lead in the class play?

Why do you feel that way?

How do you feel when your dad tells you he loves you?

What do you say?

_____

_____

_____

How do you feel when you have to practice the piano?

What can you do?

_____

_____

_____

How do you feel when you're eating dinner at a friend's house and the food tastes yucky?

What can you do about it?

_____

_____

_____

How do you feel when a kid pushes you in line at school?

What can you do?

How do you feel when you're lost in a shopping mall?

What could you do?

_____

_____

_____

How do you feel when someone wants to borrow your new baseball glove?

What do you do?

_____

_____

_____

FEELINGS FACES

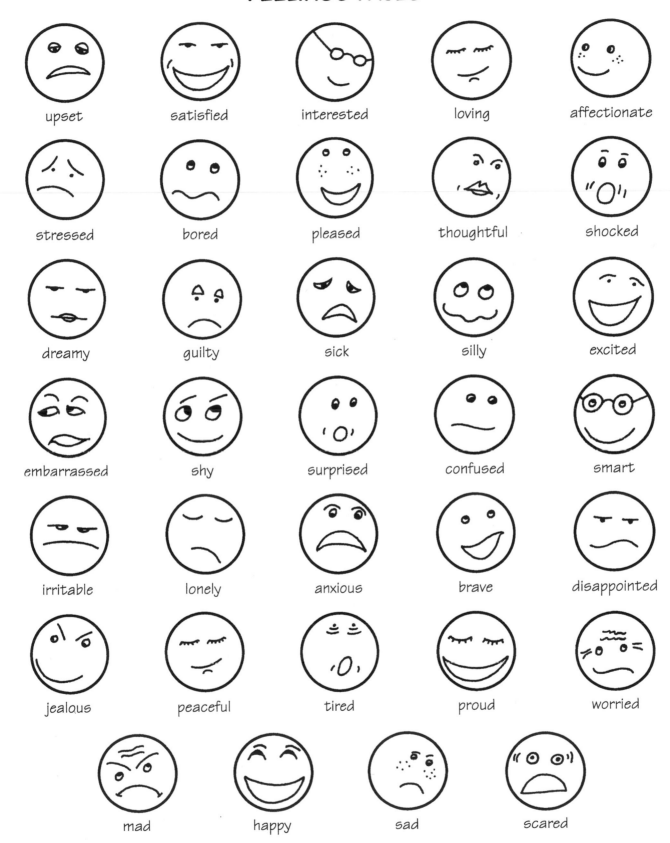

About the Author:
Lawrence E. Shapiro, Ph.D. has had more than fifteen years working with children as a teacher, school psychologist, director of a school for special-needs children, and in private practice. He is the author of over fifteen books and has invented over a dozen psychological games. Dr. Shapiro is the president of the Childswork/Childsplay catalogue, the country's largest distributor of psychologically-oriented toys, games and books.

About the Artist:
Jille Mandel was trained as an illustrator and photographer. She works at Tyler School of Art and resides in Elkins Park, Pennsylvania.